DARING HEISTS

Real Tales of Sensational Robberies and Robbers

TOM MCCARTHY

Nomad Press
A division of Nomad Communications
10 9 8 7 6 5 4 3 2 1

This book was manufactured by CGB Printers,
North Mankato, Minnesota, United States
May 2017, Job #221360
ISBN Softcover: 978-1-61930-535-9
ISBN Hardcover: 978-1-61930-531-1

Educational Consultant, Marla Conn

Questions regarding the ordering of this book should be addressed to
Nomad Press
2456 Christian St.
White River Junction, VT 05001
www.nomadpress.net

Printed in the United States.

MIX
Paper from
responsible sources
FSC
www.fsc.org   FSC® C008080

Contents

More titles in the
Mystery & Mayhem Series

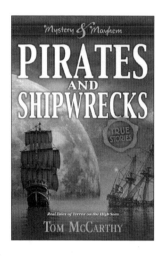

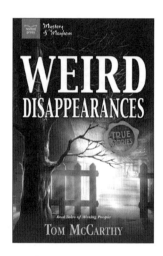

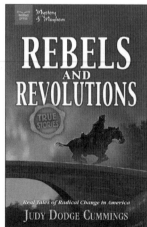

Introduction

Sensational Robberies and Robbers

We all know stealing is wrong. So why an entire book about thieves and thefts?

What drives a person to steal? Is it the thrill of the chase? Desperation? A love of puzzles? The men and women in this collection of stories have lots of different reasons for pulling off some of the biggest and most imaginative robberies in history.

The heists in this book required skill and ambition and intelligence. Bravery, too, because the thieves knew if they were caught, they'd spend a lot of time in prison. Some of the people you will read about ended up in jail. Some didn't.

The man who called himself D.B. Cooper was a planner. He knew what he was doing, right down to picking the right airplane to hijack. He knew how to jump from a speeding jet in the middle of the night over a dark and mountainous forest.

When he jumped, he had two knapsacks filled with cash that he had demanded from Northwest Airlines. The very next day, the police, FBI, and the military began a search that lasted more than 40 years and turned up only new mysteries. D.B. Cooper has never been found.

The men who robbed the Royal Mail train of millions of dollars in 1963 were planners, too. They planned the robbery for months. A gang member rode the train and studied how it was guarded. They bought a hideout and radios and a big truck to haul the money away after the robbery. They were quiet about it.

What later became known as the Great Train Robbery was so surprising people are still talking about it today, more than 50 years later.

What about Marm Mandelbaum? For more than 25 years, she led a gang that frustrated both the police and the famous Pinkerton National Detective Agency. They knew she was receiving thousands of dollars worth of jewelry and money stolen from the wealthiest people in New York City. But they could never catch her in the act.

You want stealthy? Take the gang who broke into Boston's Isabella Stewart Gardner Museum in 1990 and stole 13 world-famous paintings worth millions. Then they disappeared. The gang was never captured and the precious art has never been found.

Art attracted another gang that broke into the National Museum of Anthropology in Mexico. They stole rare gold, jade, turquoise, and obsidian artifacts from ancient Mexican civilizations, a collection worth more money than anyone could imagine. The police thought these crooks had to have been cultured and educated to want to steal these artifacts. However, the police were wrong—they were shocked by the people who turned out to have pulled off the heist.

Let's take a walk through the seamy underworld of thieves.

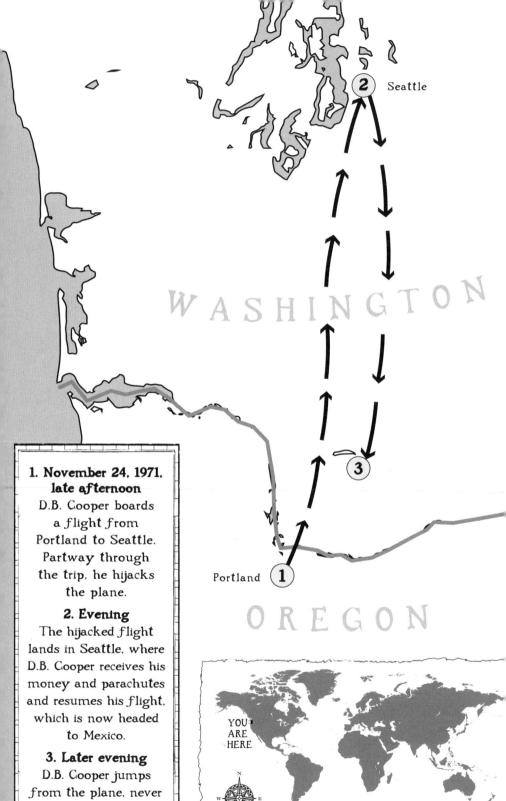

WASHINGTON

OREGON

② Seattle

③

Portland ①

1. November 24, 1971, late afternoon
D.B. Cooper boards a flight from Portland to Seattle. Partway through the trip, he hijacks the plane.

2. Evening
The hijacked flight lands in Seattle, where D.B. Cooper receives his money and parachutes and resumes his flight, which is now headed to Mexico.

3. Later evening
D.B. Cooper jumps from the plane, never to be seen again.

YOU
ARE
HERE

N
W E
S

Chapter One

D.B. Cooper: Into Thin Air

It was mid-afternoon at the busy Portland
International Airport in Oregon on
Wednesday, November 24, 1971.

A man carrying a black briefcase and wearing a
dark suit walked up to the counter of Northwest
Orient Airlines. He purchased a one-way
ticket to Seattle, an hour's flight by jet over the
mountainous and thick forest of the Pacific
Northwest. The man told the ticket agent his
name was Dan Cooper.

Dan Cooper, the man who would later become known as D.B. Cooper, was among tens of thousands of people across the country trying to get home for the holiday. The next day was Thanksgiving, followed by the long, relaxing holiday weekend. Just about everyone in the country was looking forward to a restful holiday with friends and family.

D.B. Cooper had other plans. Resting and relaxing weren't going to be a part of his Thanksgiving holiday weekend.

It is only 173 miles from Portland to Seattle. On a jet, the trip is a short hop. D.B. Cooper had to act quickly to get his plan to work.

After he bought his ticket, he joined a small group of people waiting for the call to board the jet, a Boeing 727-100. When the flight was announced at 4 p.m., he walked calmly onto the plane and sat near the rear, in seat 15D. No one else sat with him—he had the row of seats to himself.

Later, eyewitnesses would say he was about 6 feet tall. People guessed he was about 40 years old. He wore a neatly pressed shirt with a collar and a black necktie held in place by a mother-of-pearl tie pin. He looked like a businessman on his way home. That's what he wanted people to think. Of course, he had other plans.

As D.B. Cooper and his fellow passengers settled in for the flight, he sat back and lit a cigarette. In 1971, smoking on airplanes was allowed. Then, he ordered a drink from the flight attendant, who was busy helping passengers settle in for the flight.

It was getting dark as the plane taxied down the runway for what everyone thought would be a routine flight north to Seattle. The temperature outside was typical for November in the Pacific Northwest, chilly at around 45 degrees. It was starting to drizzle.

Including the crew and D.B. Cooper, there were 42 people on board. Their lives would never be the same.

One can only guess what was going through D.B. Cooper's mind as the plane lifted through the clouds and headed north. Was he crazy?

Did he know what he was doing? Or was he just hoping for the best? Since that day, everyone who has chased D.B. Cooper has said that he planned his exploit right down to the finest detail.

D.B. Cooper knew exactly what he was doing, they all say.

It was no coincidence that the Boeing 727-100 had a door at the back, with a stairway that could be lowered. It was no coincidence that the three jet engines that powered the plane were placed high on the fuselage. The engines were not level with doorways, as on some passenger jets that had the engines on their wings.

As the plane leveled off after its ascent, D.B. Cooper called the flight attendant to his seat and handed her a note on a neatly folded piece of paper. Busy settling the other passengers, she put it in her pocket and forgot about it.

A moment later, he called her back. Later, she could recall his exact, polite words.

"Miss, you had better look at my note. I have a bomb."

Startled, she stared at the man in the nice suit. He briefly opened the briefcase on his lap, just enough to let her catch a glimpse of what was inside. Packed neatly in the leather case were eight red cylinders, attached by wires to what looked like batteries. D.B. Cooper quickly and calmly closed the briefcase.

Alarmed, she pulled the note from her pocket and read.

It was printed neatly in capital letters, written with a felt-tip pen. Its message was clear and chilling. The polite man in the business suit wanted $200,000 in $20 bills and four parachutes. He also wanted to have the jet refueled as soon as possible after their arrival in Seattle.

She read the note, turned, and walked quickly to the cockpit. She had to tell the pilot that there was a change in plans. When she returned to D.B. Cooper, he was wearing dark sunglasses.

The pilot spoke over the intercom and told the passengers there would be a bit of a delay once they got to Seattle. D.B. Cooper sat back in his seat. His plan was set in motion.

It takes a lot of phone calls to meet the kind of demands that D.B. Cooper made in his note. It was not as if the president of Northwest Orient Airlines had $200,000 in $20 bills and some parachutes in his office closet.

While the plane was still in the air heading to Seattle, phone calls went out to local banks and a skydiving school as officials tried to collect what D.B. Cooper wanted. The police and the FBI were also notified. There was no time to lose. They all wanted to stop this madman on the plane.

D.B. Cooper told the nervous crew that he wanted to go to Mexico after stopping in Seattle for the loot.

In Seattle, agents from the FBI quickly pulled together the money from several Seattle-area banks—$200,000 in $20 bills. Then they found some parachutes.

The plane landed shortly after 5:30 p.m. D.B. Cooper ordered the pilot to taxi to an isolated area of the Seattle airport. Then he waited. A short while later, a man approached the back stairs of the waiting plane and delivered a knapsack jammed with the cash. He also handed over the parachutes.

Once he was satisfied that everything was in order, D.B. Cooper told the pilot he could let the other passengers leave. The nervous and relieved passengers walked quickly from the plane onto the dark tarmac.

The first part of the plan had worked perfectly. The next part would be a bit more challenging.

While the jet was being refueled, D.B. Cooper explained his plan to the flight crew. He wanted to head south to Mexico at an altitude of 10,000 feet, as slowly as the jet could fly without stalling.

This was a strange request.

Why didn't D.B. Cooper want to get away as fast as he could?

Of course, the pilot and co-pilot agreed to do what this strange man asked. It did not seem wise to argue with a man who carried a briefcase full of dynamite.

Shortly after 7:40 that night, the plane took off. On board were the pilot, two assistants, and the flight attendant. And, of course, D.B. Cooper. As the plane lifted off the tarmac and headed south, two jet fighters from a nearby air force base followed.

After takeoff, D.B. Cooper told everyone to cram into the cockpit and stay there. He had a plan and it did not include anyone watching him carry it out. At 8 p.m., a warning light in the cockpit began flashing. It was telling everyone that someone had opened the rear stairway.

As they stared at the flashing light, the nervous group felt the rear of the plane jerk up quickly. It was the same feeling you get when someone springs from a diving board. Another warning light flashed. The air pressure inside the plane had dropped. They waited an instant to calm their nerves, then ran to the back.

D.B. Cooper, his briefcase, the knapsack filled with money, and two of the parachutes were gone. Somewhere over the darkened forests of Washington, the man known as D.B. Cooper had disappeared.

No one has seen or heard from him since.

Remember, he chose to hijack an airplane that had a door at the back, with a stairway that could be lowered. The plane's jet engines were placed in a way that someone could jump out without getting sucked into the whirring blades. It was all part of D.B. Cooper's master plan.

Jumping from the rear of a jet that's flying almost 200 miles an hour is not a walk in the park. It's like jumping face first from a speeding car into a brick wall. The jumper could even be knocked unconscious. This makes it impossible to pull the rip cord on a parachute.

On top of that challenge, it was dark. And it was raining and windy and the landscape below was mountainous and thickly forested. In the best of times, say in broad daylight, it would be hard enough to steer the parachute to a place the skydiver could land safely.

But D.B. Cooper had left nothing to chance. He knew how to jump from airplanes and he knew how to land properly. No doubt he knew how to hold onto the knapsack containing the money.

The investigation started immediately after the startled crew realized D.B. Cooper had jumped. A quick radio call to headquarters sent teams of FBI agents and special investigators into a frenzy of activity.

A crazy man was somewhere in the forest with $200,000 of Northwest Orient Airline's money. He had threated the lives of 41 people and a million dollar aircraft. He had disrupted the Thanksgiving plans of hundreds of people.

D.B. Cooper had to be caught.

When the plane landed, FBI agents swarmed aboard. They quickly recovered 66 fingerprints that could have come from the man known as D.B. Cooper. They also found his tie, the tie pin, and two of the four parachutes.

Next, they rounded up as many eyewitnesses as they could find. They quickly developed a sketch of what the man looked like and sent it to newspapers and television stations.

There was no time to waste.

The southwest corner of Washington state is covered with magnificent trees. Douglas firs, Sitka spruces, and hardwoods grow to massive sizes in the rich soil and rainy climate. For the people who live there, the forest provides a way of life—most people work harvesting lumber.

It is also hunting and fishing country, with an abundance of mountain elk, bear, cougars, coyotes, and even wild dogs. In spring and summer, it is impossible to walk 10 yards through the woods without spotting a raccoon, badger skunk, or squirrel. There are hundreds of streams, ponds, and lakes where the fishing is very good.

For someone who knows the ways of the woods and forests, it is a welcoming environment that offers safety and many places to hide. For hundreds of law enforcement officers and FBI agents, it was a nightmare.

These men should have been sitting down with their families to a nice turkey dinner. Instead, they were climbing slippery, muddy slopes hoping for the impossible—a clue to where D.B. Cooper might be.

The biggest problem was that no one knew precisely when D.B. Cooper had jumped from the jet. Investigators only knew when the flight crew felt the plane's back end pop up into the air. At 200 miles an hour, that made it difficult to estimate what area the plane was flying over.

Also, the heavy winds could have blown a man in a parachute miles as he drifted to the ground. The crew onboard the Northwest jet and the FBI could not come up with an accurate estimate of where D.B. Cooper might have landed. The jet pilots from the air force base who had been following the plane never saw D.B Cooper jump.

The best they could figure is that D.B. Cooper landed in the isolated wilderness by the Lewis River in southwestern Washington. Beginning the

next day, Thanksgiving Day, law enforcement officers began to go door to door and talk to local farmers. No one had seen a thing.

A composite sketch of D.B. Cooper by the FBI.

FBI agents do not give up on cases. D.B. Cooper had to be somewhere. He had to have made a mistake at some point. Maybe he left a clue behind in the forest.

But as we have learned, D.B. Cooper was not a man to leave anything to chance. Apparently, his plan included simply disappearing into thin air.

In early 1972, a few months after the hijacking, the weather turned warm and the ground thawed. The FBI took up the search in the mountains again. This time, they brought a huge group of trackers, including soldiers from a nearby army base and local volunteers. They combed the woods for more than two weeks.

They found nothing.

They tried again in April, for another 18 days. Nothing again. The search for D.B. Cooper consumed the FBI and other law enforcement officials for years. Some say that looking for D.B. Cooper was the most expensive search in American history. During all those man hours, did any evidence surface?

Since the day D.B. Cooper jumped into history, the FBI has processed more than a thousand suspects. Some even claimed to be D.B. Cooper himself. They were all ruled out as people who wanted attention, even if it was bad attention.

In 1978, a hunter found the torn remains of a small card. It contained instructions for lowering the stairs of a Boeing 727. Could this have belonged to D.B. Cooper?

In 1980, a young boy on vacation with his family on the Columbia River was digging in the loose sand on the edge of the riverbank. Three packets of money rolled from the dirt.

The bundles of bills were badly deteriorated, but they were determined to be some of D.B. Cooper's ransom money! The bundles were still held together with the rubber bands that had been wrapped around the money before it was given to D.B. Cooper. The rotting bills were the first evidence to emerge in the nine years since D.B. Cooper bailed out of the plane.

But where was the rest of the money? Where was D.B. Cooper?

In 1981, a human skull was unearthed along that same riverbank. It was found during excavations in search of additional evidence in the case.

Might it belong to D.B. Cooper? Could he have been dead during all these years of searching? Forensic scientists determined that it belonged to a woman, possibly of Native American ancestry.

In 1988, a portion of a parachute was pulled from the Columbia River. Tests showed it was not D.B. Cooper's. In 2008, a group of children found another parachute. Again, results showed it had nothing to do with D.B. Cooper. Every time, though, people who were still following the case got their hopes up.

No one—not a single person in 45 years—ever reported that a family member matching D.B. Cooper's description had disappeared that day. No one ever called the FBI to report that a fellow worker didn't show up again after the hijacking. No neighbors called to say that the man who lived next door had never returned home.

Do you think this is strange?

If someone simply vanished, someone else would say something. This would be especially true when the strange case of D.B. Cooper was in the news night and day, week in and week out.

The FBI finally officially suspended its search for D.B. Cooper in July 2016.

How about this theory?

D.B. Cooper, always the careful planner, chose the long, four-day Thanksgiving weekend for his adventure on purpose. With those extra days, he could hijack the plane, grab the money, parachute into the forest, walk out, and returned to normal life, with a bit more money than before.

It's fun to imagine him returning to work that following Monday.

"How was your weekend?" a fellow worker might ask. "Hope you had time to relax a bit."

"It was great," the man known as D.B. Cooper replies. "I got outside and did some hiking. I'm glad I did. It was quite rewarding."

WHAT ELSE WAS HAPPENING IN 1971?

- In January, the U.S. government bans cigarette advertisements on television.

- The television show *All in the Family* debuts on television and becomes famous for being the first show during which a toilet is flushed.

- Airplane hijacking is more common during this time period than today. Why? In the 1960s and 1970s, there are few security measures for passengers to go through.

NEW YORK

Upper
Manhattan

EAST RIVER

Lower Manhattan

NEW
JERSEY

HUDSON RIVER

Brooklyn

1800s
Fredericka "Marm"
Mandelbaum presides
over an extensive
ring of thieves in
lower Manhattan in
New York City, until
she flees to Canada
to escape the police.

YOU ARE
HERE

N
W E
S

Chapter Two

The Queen of Thieves

A warm, gentle breeze lifted the clatter of
voices above the crowded sidewalk. Peddlers
shouted for attention in English and German
and Yiddish as wisps of smoke from cooking
fires mingled almost deliciously with the
sharper smells of horse droppings and hay.

Fredericka Mandelbaum smiled to herself as she
stepped slowly from her shop into the throng of
passersby moving quickly along Clinton Street
in New York City. Her business was doing very
well and she was happy about that.

There were so many bustling people on the sidewalk. When Fredericka Mandelbaum entered the throng, she was swept along like a bobbing twig in a fast-moving stream. Fredericka Mandelbaum was more than 6 feet tall and weighed almost 250 pounds, so seeing her being moved quickly along the sidewalk was something to behold!

Many of the people she passed on the street smiled back at her. They knew her as a kind and friendly shop owner.

She wasn't.

Fredericka Mandelbaum had business associates with names like Boiled Oysters Malloy, Gyp the Blood, and Hell-Cat Maggie. This last one filed her teeth to sharp points and had brass fingernails.

Fredericka Mandelbaum knew guys named Gallus Mag and Scotchy Lavelle. Gallus Mag owned a saloon. He would bite off the ears of annoying customers and keep them in a pickle jar above the bar.

There was a special place in Fredericka Mandelbaum's heart for pickpockets with names such as Black Lena Kleinschmidt, Big Mary, Ellen Clegg, Queen Liz, Little Annie, Old Mother Hubbard, and Kid Glove Rose.

These oddly named people knew Fredericka Mandelbaum as the "Queen of Thieves." And for good reason.

Fredericka Mandelbaum's neighbors called her "Marm." She had a round face with full cheeks that at times made her look almost angelic, like a loving grandmother. But appearances can be deceiving. In fact, Marm Mandelbaum counted on appearances being deceiving. She figured that the fewer the people who knew what she was really up to, the better.

That was especially true about the police.

The same morning that Marm Mandelbaum stepped into the street and smiled to herself about her good fortune, a group of detectives was putting the finishing touches on a plan. They were going to catch her red-handed.

The famous Pinkerton detectives had been following Marm Mandelbaum for months. They wanted nothing more than to put the kindly looking shop owner in prison for a very long time.

The 1884 contest of wits between Marm Mandelbaum and the best detectives in the country still has people talking.

Some people who knew Marm Mandelbaum described her as "mountainous," but she didn't care. That was the magic of Marm Mandelbaum. She knew how to blend in with her surroundings despite her size and the flamboyant hats with long and colorful feathers she loved to wear.

Marm Mandelbaum had a fortune in stolen goods hidden away in warehouses in New York City. She was confident that no one would ever catch her.

She was a walking mystery—a woman of opposites—and she liked it that way. She was proud of her size and did nothing to hide it. To the people in her Lower East Side neighborhood, she appeared to be a kindly businesswoman. The police knew she was a master thief, but could never catch her. She loved money, but lived in a small apartment above her store. She was very smart, but liked being thought of as a simple storeowner.

Marm Mandelbaum was a phenomenon. She was a master criminal who had so much stolen property she needed two large warehouses to hold it.

Thieves from across the entire United States sought her out when they wanted to sell stolen diamond rings and ruby necklaces, silver candelabras or ornate chandeliers. Marm Mandelbaum could get money for anything. One day, she even bought a herd of stolen sheep from halfway across the country in Chicago!

Thieves knew Marm Mandelbaum would pay for the loot and not ask questions about where it came from. They knew Marm Mandelbaum would never talk to police or turn them in. They knew she would help them escape if the need arose, and maybe even hire lawyers to help them.

That's why they called her the Queen of Thieves and treated her with so much respect.

Marm Mandelbaum was powerful and calm and wise. Thieves marveled at Marm Mandelbaum's ability to escape the attention of the police and the district attorney, who wanted more than anything to send her to jail.

By 1880, at the height of her power, she bought and sold millions of dollars of stolen goods. It was an odd occupation for a woman who pretended to be a simple shopkeeper. It was the sort of occupation that will attract the attention of the police, at least some of them, who want to put thieves in jail.

But they couldn't. And that is what drove them crazy.

Marm Mandelbaum was too wily to get caught. She paid judges and police to look the other way. She paid a small fortune to lawyers to keep her out of trouble if she ever had to go to court.

That's where the Pinkerton National Detective Agency comes into Marm's story. These were the most famous investigators in the history of the United States.

Pinkerton detectives could not be bribed like other detectives in New York City. They always got the criminals they chased.

Before the Pinkerton National Detective Agency went after Marm Mandelbaum, they had helped capture famous bank robbers and thieves across the country.

But Marm Mandelbaum was different. She might have been the smartest criminal in all of New York City and maybe even the United States. Marm Mandelbaum seemed to have no weaknesses. She had everything under control and knew how to deal with it.

How did she get like that?

Marm Mandelbaum had come to New York City in 1848 from Germany. She was a poor immigrant with no money. But she did have ambition and a total lack of fear. When the rusty steamship carrying the young Fredericka Mandelbaum docked in New York City, she took a deep breath and smiled. Even the air smelled different in America—it smelled of hope.

Marm Mandelbaum settled in an area in the lower part of Manhattan called Little Germany. If you were poor and German in 1848, that's where you went.

Little Germany was crowded and grim. Shabby apartments were packed tightly with thousands of other people who had moved to New York City hoping for a new chance. But the crowded streets and overflowing rooms had something Germany did not have—a glimmer of hope.

Marm saw that glimmer and seized it the moment she moved into a tiny, two-room apartment, which she shared with two other families. Everyone slept on the floor and took turns cooking.

With so many people crammed into such a small space, it was difficult to breathe. To make things worse, the stench of a nearby slaughterhouse penetrated everything.

On her first morning in New York, Marm Mandelbaum walked outside as the sun rose between two darkened buildings across Clinton Street. It was already noisy. Horses were snorting, and peddlers sang out praises for their wares. She noticed children scavenging for bits of coal to burn to ward off the early morning chill.

Things seemed strange but exciting.

Marm Mandelbaum soon discovered that no more than three miles from her table on Clinton Street lived some of the wealthiest people in the world. She sometimes walked up Fifth Avenue and studied the stately brick townhouses with grand entrances and doormen. She stared admiringly at the ornate horse-drawn carriages that waited in tree-lined driveways. She craned her neck to look up at the tall buildings on Park Avenue and wondered what splendor they held.

These homes were glorious in a way she could only imagine. There were 20-room apartments filled with plush furniture that had been hand-crafted from exotic woods. There were walls lined with art from the most famous artists, drawers filled with jewelry, long tables topped with gold and silver candelabras, and windows shaded by intricate silk draperies. There was valuable silverware and priceless plates made from the finest porcelain.

Interesting, she thought, as she turned and headed back downtown to Little Germany. This is the opportunity I have been looking for. This is my chance.

Marm Mandelbaum noticed small things that others did not. She saw that the young children in the streets did more than scamper for bits of coal. Some of the darting children had a knack for picking pockets. They could quickly remove money and valuables from distracted passersby.

One afternoon, she watched a young girl bump into a stranger who was walking down Clinton Street. When the startled man jumped back, the young girl reached into his left front coat pocket, pulled a watch from it, and just as quickly darted way. It happened in less than three seconds, and the man did not notice a thing.

Later that afternoon, the young girl walked boldly up to Marm Mandelbaum.

"Would you like to buy a watch?" she asked.

"I know where you got that watch," Marm Mandelbaum said. "But I don't mind."

Marm Mandelbaum bought the watch for 25 cents, far less than it was worth. Later that afternoon, she sold it for $2.

Soon, word spread that Marm Mandelbaum would buy anything. And she would not ask questions about where it came from or how it had been obtained.

And so it began.

Marm Mandelbaum's business began slowly and grew, but this was not your normal business, of course. She had one rule: If you treat your customers well, they will return. And, boy, did Marm Mandelbaum's customers return.

Soon Marm Mandelbaum had made enough money selling stolen goods to open a store in a ramshackle building at the corner of Clinton and Rivington Streets in Little Germany. From the outside, anyone walking down the street saw a store that sold fabrics, housewares, plates, and other things to set up an apartment in New York City.

What people wouldn't see was the back room.

She filled the room with stolen goods. Most had been lifted in the dark of night from the uptown apartments of wealthy New Yorkers.

Marm Mandelbaum had a stonemason build a false chimney with a hidden door leading into this secret storeroom. If the police or a detective made a visit to the store, she could quickly toss her stolen loot through the secret door.

Marm Mandelbaum often gave to local charities and was generous to her neighbors. She thought to herself, "I am a special Ma because I give them what a normal mother cannot sometimes give—money and horses and diamonds."

Then she smiled as she considered her good fortune. How much things had changed since those dark days in Germany! "It takes brains to be a real lady," she thought.

But such bravura could not last, even for the charmed Marm Mandelbaum. There is an old expression that says if you play with fire, you eventually get burned. Marm Mandelbaum and her hidden wealth began to attract the attention of some people who could not be bribed.

As she grew bolder, she became less careful. Marm Mandelbaum was impressed by a man named George Leslie, who came to New York looking for excitement. He soon assembled a gang of thieves and they started robbing banks.

Marm Mandelbaum helped George Leslie in his robberies. He robbed the Manhattan Savings Institution of about $3 million and Marm Mandelbaum got some of that money for her help. *The New York Times* newspaper called it "the most sensational in the history of bank robberies in this country."

That's the sort of thing that will attract the attention of police.

Marm Mandelbaum also joined forces with a suave art thief named Adam Worth, who happened to be under watch of the police. That was her next mistake.

Adam Worth's gang included "Piano" Charley, a jewel thief and a train robber. There was also Scratch Becker, a master forger, who could make anything look real.

As her plans and schemes grew and expanded, Marm Mandelbaum attracted more attention. Many police were honest, and she could not bribe them like she usually did. They turned to their boss, the district attorney, and pleaded with him to arrest Marm Mandelbaum. The fact that she was thriving in New York was getting embarrassing.

Marm Mandelbaum's first sign of trouble was a man named James Scott.

This storeowner from Boston had been robbed and was angry about it. He told police that someone had stolen 26 cashmere shawls worth $780 from his store on Washington Street in Boston. In addition to that, he claimed, the thieves also took off with 2,000 yards of black silk worth $4,000. That's more than a mile of expensive fabric!

James Scott had reason to believe that his goods ended up in the possession of one Fredericka Mandelbaum of New York City.

Soon enough, police made their way to Marm Mandelbaum's store. She protested her innocence. Her lawyers pointed out to the judge that she was nothing but a businesswoman with a small store on Clinton Street. Marm Mandelbaum was allowed to go free.

But in 1884, James Scott's claims finally made the district attorney pay attention. He knew there were very few police and judges he could trust— so many of them were on her payroll! So the district attorney turned to the famous Pinkerton National Detective Agency and asked them to sneak into Marm Mandelbaum's very secretive organization.

Why was the Pinkerton National Detective Agency so famous? Because they were successful. The Pinkertons were like dogs with bones when they got wind of a criminal who needed to be caught. They were so successful that the agency still exists today, more than 150 years after it was first started.

Once the Pinkerton detectives infiltrated Marm Mandelbaum's circle of thieves, they learned something useful. Sure, Marm Mandelbaum enjoyed the diamonds and the gold and silver vases her people had stolen for her. She liked the money and the glorious sparkling jewelry.

But the Pinkerton detectives learned that what really made Marm Mandelbaum's heart skip a beat was silk. She loved silk.

Silk was Marm Mandelbaum's weakness.

The Pinkertons set a trap that even the wily Marm Mandelbaum could not avoid. Knowing she had a weakness for silk, they put a special mark on a roll of precious and rare silk from Asia—a small red star. Then they made it known on the street that the roll of silk was stored in a small warehouse in Little Germany, not far from Marm Mandelbaum's apartment.

When Marm Mandelbaum heard of this rare silk, she arranged for it to be stolen. Soon, the roll of exotic fabric was in her secret storage room behind her Clinton Street store. The theft was a rare mistake for Marm Mandelbaum.

One of the Pinkerton detectives, who prided himself on his appearance, stopped shaving. He waited for three weeks to let his dark beard grow long and scruffy. Then, he stopped bathing and found some ragged clothing. He looked very much like the thieves who dealt with Marm Mandelbaum.

Happy with his appearance, he went to her store. He mentioned very quietly that he wanted to buy some silk, noting that he would pay top dollar for it.

Marm Mandelbaum fell for the guise hook, line, and sinker. The Pinkerton trap closed on her in a flash. When she showed the Pinkerton detective the fabric, he quickly found the small red star they had marked on the silk. Marm Mandelbaum was caught red-handed.

Marm Mandelbaum's arrest caused a sensation in New York City. Her photograph was on the front page of every newspaper in the city. When she was taken to court for her first appearance, there was a mob outside, hoping to get a glimpse of this mysterious woman.

"I am innocent," she told the judge. "I am a simple businesswoman who has operated a store on Clinton Street for 35 years."

The judge, a regular guest at her festive dinners, agreed and allowed her to post bail to go free until her trial. She gathered her papers and her dignity and walked from the courtroom.

The crowds outside separated to let her pass. She did not look up. She had other things on her mind. The trial would not go well, she knew. The Pinkertons had caught her. All the elegant dinners could not prevent her from going to jail.

But Marm Mandelbaum had a plan.

She headed north from the courthouse to Clinton Street, but instead of stopping at her apartment, she kept going. She did not stop until she reached Canada, where the police could not arrest her. She arranged for several of her gang members to meet her in Hamilton, Ontario. They brought her more than $1 million from her stash of stolen money.

She stayed there for the rest of her life, safe from the prying eyes of detectives.

The Queen of Thieves

Marm Mandelbaum lived well in Hamilton, but she was homesick. She missed her beloved apartment on Clinton Street and her adoring neighbors. Marm Mandelbaum died in 1895, a sad woman.

Before she died, she begged her friends to bury her in New York City. If she could not live out her final days in her beloved Little Germany, at least she could be put to rest there.

When Marm Mandelbaum's body returned for burial, it caused quite a sensation. Her funeral was crowded. Throngs of her grieving supporters expressed their love and sadness at the passing of such a kind woman.

Not everyone was sad, though. As Marm Mandelbaum's funeral procession worked its way slowly down Clinton Street, more than a dozen of her former students worked their way up the street. They smiled as they picked the pockets of the unsuspecting and curious mourners.

Marm would have been very proud.

WHAT ELSE WAS HAPPENING IN THE MID-1800S?

- The safety pin is invented in 1849.

- The California Gold Rush starts in 1849. The discovery of gold brings large numbers of fortune seekers to the American West.

- The devastating American Civil War between the Northern and Southern states begins in 1861. It would not end until 1865.

- President Abraham Lincoln issues the Emancipation Proclamation in 1863, declaring all slaves to be free.

- The United States buys Alaska from Russia in 1867.

- The first successful oil well in the United States is drilled in Titusville, Pennsylvania, in 1859.

- President Lincoln is assassinated in 1865.

- The Transcontinental Railroad, the first railroad line across the entire country, is completed in 1869.

- The can opener is invented in 1870.

- The first telephone call is made in 1876, when inventor Alexander Graham Bell says to his assistant, "Mr. Watson, come here."

- Thomas Edison switches on the first electric light in 1879.

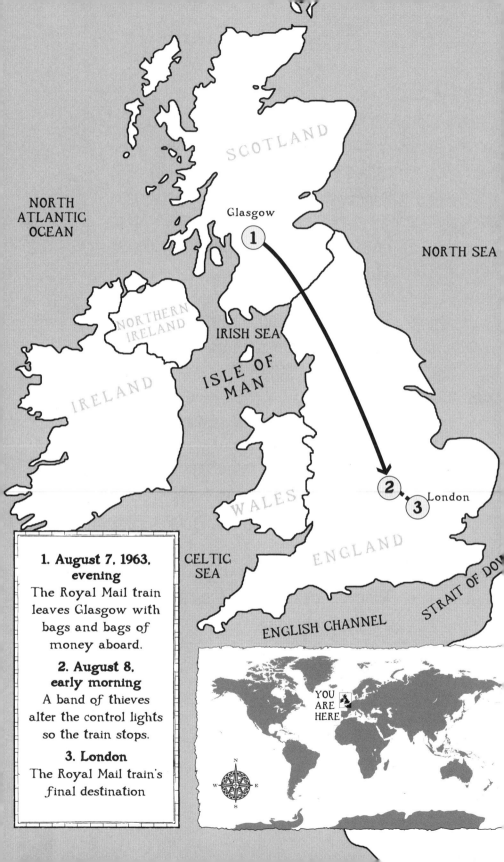

NORTH
ATLANTIC
OCEAN

SCOTLAND

Glasgow

1

NORTH SEA

NORTHERN
IRELAND

IRISH SEA

ISLE OF
MAN

IRELAND

WALES

2 **3** London

CELTIC
SEA

ENGLAND

STRAIT OF DOV

ENGLISH CHANNEL

**1. August 7, 1963,
evening**
The Royal Mail train
leaves Glasgow with
bags and bags of
money aboard.

**2. August 8,
early morning**
A band of thieves
alter the control lights
so the train stops.

3. London
The Royal Mail train's
final destination

YOU
ARE
HERE

Chapter Three

The Great Train Robbery

The Royal Mail train left platform 11 at Glasgow Central Station shortly before 7 p.m. on August 7, 1963. It was a warm and cloudy night. A man watched as the powerful engine and its 12 cars began to pick up speed through the outskirts of Glasgow and head south into the Scottish countryside.

As it slowly faded into the darkness, the man on the platform placed a long-distance telephone call to London. His message to the band of thieves on the other end of the call: The train has left the station—time to get moving.

Several months earlier, a casual remark grew into an idea to rob the Royal Mail train. Word spread among a group of thieves in London about the huge amount of money the train sometimes carried.

A quiet whisper grew louder as it spread from one man to another in the close-knit community of London thieves. Soon, 15 Englishmen were working very hard on plans to steal the money from the Royal Mail train and get it into their pockets.

They knew this would not be an ordinary robbery.

Every successful robbery needs a mastermind, a man or a woman who knows the right people and knows how to get things done. In this case, there were several masterminds.

A man named Bruce Reynolds was the first to hear about the Royal Mail train and its sacks full of money. Bruce Reynolds called some friends, including Charlie Wilson, Roy James, Gordon Goody, Buster Edwards, and Ronnie Biggs.

These men, all from London, were not what you would call Boy Scouts. They were all enthusiastic thieves, and when they heard about the Royal Mail train, they became even more excited. Maybe it was the challenge of robbing a train that was so exciting.

Robbing a train is different from robbing a bank. Whether it is in a shopping mall or standing on the corner of a city street, a bank stays in the same place. It doesn't move. A thief can study it from a distance. They can walk around and look for places to break in. They can study the guards and learn when they take breaks. Then the thieves can figure out when and how to pull off the robbery.

Trains move, and they move fast.

It is difficult to stop them. A robber can't just flag down a train and jump aboard. The London thieves all knew how to rob banks, but a train was a special challenge.

First, the gang members did their homework. They studied the Royal Mail train and its route. They asked questions about guards, locks, and alarms.

How many times did the train stop on its 450-mile trip from Scotland to London? They looked for weak spots. The thieves were not worried when they learned that, in 125 years of carrying money, the Royal Mail train had never been robbed.

If anything, this fact made the thieves more determined to try. Some people in the robbery business know it is often best to do the unexpected.

The London thieves knew they'd need a way to stop the train. The trip from Glasgow to London was long, and at times the train went streaking down the tracks at 80 miles an hour. Where was the best place to pull off a robbery? Where did the train slow down?

They had heard there was so much money on the train that they would need a truck to haul it all away. Where could they get a truck? They knew from experience that once they robbed the train, alarms would sound and the police would soon be swarming the countryside.

Where could they hide?

One of the group, pretending to be a schoolteacher, spent two months riding the train and making friends with the workers. He gained inside knowledge on how things were done and looked for weak spots.

The gang leaders picked the place to pull off the robbery—a tiny dot called Sears Crossing. It lay between the villages of Oakley and Brill in the English county of Buckinghamshire. The train would have to slow down as it passed through.

Another man in the group bought a rundown farm named Leatherslade, about 27 miles from Sears Crossing. Leatherslade was on a deserted hillside that few people ever passed by. It was perfect for a hideout!

Two others in the gang bought a truck and two Land Rovers. These would be used to carry the bags of stolen money.

By early August, they were ready. Everything was in place and the time was ripe. The banks had been closed for a few days, which meant the Royal Mail train would be carrying more money than usual. Their biggest ally was surprise.

As they waited for the train to leave Glasgow, the 15 men were nervous but excited. If things worked according to plan, the Royal Mail's 125-year streak of safe cash delivery would be over before the sun came up.

The new and powerful engine warmed up at platform 11 at Glasgow's Central Station. Workers in the 12 cars were bustling. As the engine purred, they separated the bags filled with cash on their way to banks in London from regular the bags of mail. They moved the bags of money and other valuables to what was called the "high-value packages" car. This car sat guarded, two cars back from the engine.

Inside this special car, the bags were stacked inside wooden cupboards that lined the walls. Then, the cupboards were padlocked. The five workers who had brought the money to the car locked themselves in, for extra safety.

Can't be too careful.

That night, there were so many bags full of cash that the workers could not fit them all into the padlocked cupboards. There were so many, in fact, that 60 bulging bags had to be stacked on the floor in the aisles. Walking through the car, workers tripped over the sacks of money. There was enough cash in that one small railroad car that it could have paid the expenses of a small country for a year.

There is an odd thing about the train and the high-value packages car that night. There were no special precautions in place for extra protection.

Several years before, the railroad had installed alarms on the high-value packages cars. They had installed bars on the windows and built a special radio center for the guards to use to call police in case of an emergency. But these things quickly became too expensive to maintain. Who would rob a train? Why spend the extra money? So they stopped the practice.

The night of August 7, 1963, the high-value car had no bars on the windows, no alarm systems, and no radio.

The robbers must have known, and it must have made them smile.

As the Royal Mail train headed toward London, the gang of thieves began working feverishly to put their plan into action. At 3 a.m., three men dressed in overalls left their hillside hideout at Leatherslade Farm in two Land Rovers and a large truck.

When they got to Sears Crossing, the men pulled a ladder from the truck. They climbed the tower that held control lights, which are like traffic lights. Train engineers use these lights to know when to speed up or slow down—or, on rare occasions, to stop completely.

One man held the ladder and listened for the approaching Royal Mail train. His accomplice covered the green light, blacking it out, then turned on a red light powered by a six-volt battery.

As the two thieves attended to their stoplight, the rest of the gang took their places on either side of the track in the darkness.

The Royal Mail train engineer, Jack Mills, must have been confused when he saw the red signal to stop. What was going on? But he stopped.

As the train slowed to a stop, the fireman climbed down from the engine to see what was going on. Jack Mills watched curiously from the engine. He went to a nearby siding, where he knew there was a telephone. He thought he would call ahead and ask why they had to stop at such a deserted place as Sears Crossing.

Reaching for the phone, he jumped back in surprise. The telephone lines had been cut. Something was not right. As he ran back to the train, he was grabbed from behind by two men and overpowered, his hands tied.

Six members of the gang climbed aboard the high-value car and forced their way in. They made the five guards to lie face down on the floor in a corner. The thieves brought the engineer and fireman into the high-value car, handcuffed them together, and put them down beside the guards.

The gang worked with the precision of a well-rehearsed platoon of Navy SEALs.

Other gang members climbed aboard the train from both sides and, soon, they were all inside the high-value car. The sight of those overflowing mail bags must have been beautiful after so many months of planning and waiting.

The London thieves knew they had only a small amount of time, no more than a half hour, to get the bags off the train. They knew also that doing this at Sears Crossing, where other trains would soon be passing by, was not a good idea.

This is where all their planning and thinking helped. One of the men unhooked the engine and the high-value car from the rest of the train. He drove this smaller train slowly to a darkened siding a half mile away.

The gang set to work. No one spoke—there was too much to do, and they had to do their work in the darkness.

In a flurry, the robbers pulled 120 bags of cash from the high-value car. By making a human chain and passing the money from one man to another right into the truck, which was parked on the siding, it was quick work. The vehicles were running for a quick escape to Leatherslade Farm.

They stuck to their 30-minute limit.

They were so disciplined that they left bags of money on the high-value car's floor when the time was up. Everyone knew that after 30 minutes, the railroad would begin to be curious why it had not heard from the Royal Mail and would call police.

With the truck loaded, the robbers jumped into the Land Rovers and headed to Leatherslade

Farm over narrow backcountry roads. Smiles slowly began to form. The first part of the plan had worked perfectly. Now, they had to avoid the police by laying low.

As they drove, they turned on a special VHF police radio they purchased for just that purpose. The gang listened for any news that word of their audacious robbery had gotten out. They did not have to wait long. Just as they were pulling into the darkened Leatherslade Farm, the radio cackled with the first report.

"A robbery has been committed and you'll never believe it—they've stolen the train!"

The police were about to start looking for them. But running around like scared chickens would only attract more attention. The thieves brought the bags of money into the main room of the farmhouse and poured it all on the floor.

Fifteen shares, one for each man. They were instant millionaires. For a moment, they sat and stared at the piles of money in front of them. It was more than they had ever seen. And it was theirs.

The thieves had a decision to make—stay at Leatherslade Farm lying low or split up and head to London right away?

In London, they had friends who would help them. But was it safe? As the discussion continued, several of the men took a break to play a game of Monopoly. Instead of using toy money, they used bills from their heist. They were giddy with success.

As the police radio came alive with more reports, the thieves knew time was short. If they were going to leave, they needed to make a decision. Soon, the police would have them surrounded, and all the money in the word would not help.

They began to disband and head out. At that moment, not a single one of the robbers suspected that they had just experienced the high point of their caper. Sitting on the floor surrounded by millions of dollars was a shining moment. But for many of the 15 men, that's all it was—a moment.

A gang is only as strong as its weakest member. The police knew it would be very hard to find the masterminds who had organized the theft from the Royal Mail train. But they also knew someone else in the gang might soon do something dumb that would attract attention.

The thieves did not disappoint.

While the London gang was counting its loot at Leatherslade Farm, police arrived at Sears Crossing with their mouths wide open. The sun was beginning to rise, as were tempers. Who would dare do such a thing? And how do we catch them?

Soon, a major search was underway. The post office was in charge of the Royal Mail train and more than a little embarrassed. It put up a reward that today would be worth more than a million dollars.

People across Great Britain woke up to the news that a Royal Mail train had been robbed of more than 2 million pounds. It was a stunning amount of money. Today, it would be worth almost 50 million pounds, or more than 66 million dollars. Newspapers and radios reported the robbery with a name that has stuck for more than 50 years: the Great Train Robbery.

No one had ever pulled off such a heist, and no one has since.

By lunchtime of the following day, the famous Scotland Yard had been called in. After a few days, investigators finally found Leatherslade Farm, but the gang was long gone. All that was left was the truck used by the robbers, which had been hastily painted yellow, as well as the Land Rovers. They also found food, bedding, sleeping bags, post-office sacks, registered mail packages, and the Monopoly game.

Investigators also found fingerprints—the first mistake the gang had made.

With those fingerprints, the chief detective, a man named Tommy Butler, could track down the gang, one man at a time. The thieves had all been arrested at some point, so they all had fingerprint records sitting in police files.

Tommy Butler was nicknamed the "Grey Fox" for his efficiency in tracking criminals. He was a hard man who worked long hours. So long, in fact, that some of the men who worked for him complained, but it did no good.

Tommy Butler was the worst kind of news for the gang. He never let up. He followed one clue after another. He talked to every person who might have heard a rumor or who might have seen a neighbor spending money in a frenzy.

He set up an investigation schedule that had detectives getting only three hours of sleep each night. Tommy Butler took the Great Train Robbery personally.

There is a certainty about criminals that police rely on. Robbers always talk about the crime. If the gang members had simply sat back and kept quiet, they might have remained free. But, soon enough, a man from South London who had heard about the robbery from a neighbor was arrested for a minor crime.

In exchange for his freedom, he told what he knew of the Great Train Robbery.

A gang member named Roger Cordrey was caught and arrested. He began to talk, and shortly after he opened his mouth, eight more of the gang members and several associates were caught.

Within six months of the robbery, 11 of the 15 robbers were locked up and awaiting trial. However, very little of the money was recovered. This made people talk and wonder—where was the loot? Much of the money was stolen by other criminals, spent on lawyers, or given to greedy relatives.

Most members of the gang spent more than 10 years in jail. Almost a year after they had so gleefully removed the sacks of money from the train, a judge sentencing the gang would call the robbery "a crime of sordid violence inspired by vast greed."

But not all the gang members suffered the same fate. With the help of some friends on the outside, Charlie Wilson escaped from Winson Green prison in Birmingham, England, in less than three minutes and disappeared into the night.

Eleven months after that, Ronnie Biggs escaped from Wandsworth Prison, 15 months into his sentence. He later fled to Paris, where he used some of his riches for plastic surgery to change how he looked.

Bruce Reynolds escaped to Mexico with his wife, Angela, and young son, Nick. They lived lavishly for a time with his share of the take. Then, he tried to find work and live honestly under false identities, first in Canada and then France. But the strain of waiting to hear the police at the door proved too much.

He returned to England and fell back into the easier money that a life of crime provided. In 1968, five years after the Great Train Robbery, he was arrested and sentenced to 25 years in jail.

Buster Edwards fled to Mexico with his family, where he lived for a while with Bruce Reynolds and later Charlie Wilson. He returned to England in 1966, when he was caught and sentenced to 15 years in jail.

They say that crime does not pay, and for the members of the gang who pulled off the Great Train Robbery, that's certainly true. Ten years in a dank and cold English prison cell is a pretty high price to pay for a few days of vast wealth.

But for a brief moment, playing Monopoly in an abandoned barn using real money to buy fake real estate, it almost seemed worth it.

WHAT ELSE WAS HAPPENING IN 1963?

- President John F. Kennedy is assassinated in Dallas, Texas, on November 22.

- On January 11, the Beatles' record *Please Please Me* becomes the biggest hit in Great Britain. By September, the rock-and-roll foursome makes its first American T.V. appearance and becomes the most popular band in the world, sparking a phenomenon called "Beatlemania."

- Russian cosmonaut Valentina V. Tereshkova becomes the first woman in space aboard a rocket called *Vostok 6*.

- The United States Postal Service begins using ZIP codes on letters and packages for the first time. The speedy name stands for Zoning Improvement Plan.

- American poet Robert Frost dies in Boston at age 88.

- In November, a new style of telephone with buttons instead of a rotary dial is introduced. Its inventors say it will make calling much easier and faster.

- McDonald's replaces its mascot, "Speedee," with a new character called Ronald McDonald.

- The British Broadcasting Corporation introduces a new television series called *Doctor Who*.

- C.S. Lewis, popular author of the Narnia books, dies in England.

- Marvel Comics introduces a new superhero called Spiderman.

- Civil rights leader Martin Luther King Jr. gives his famous "I Have a Dream" speech to more than 250,000 people gathered on the wide mall near the Lincoln Memorial in Washington, DC.

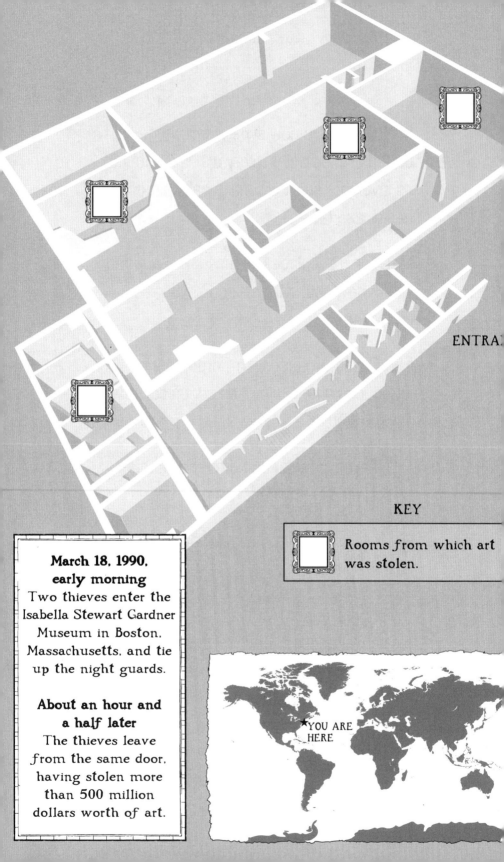

ENTRA[NCE]

KEY

Rooms from which art was stolen.

★ YOU ARE HERE

Chapter Four

A Half Billion Dollar Heist

The night watchman was startled by the short burst of the buzzer at the side door. It was nearly 1:30 in the morning. Even during the day, it was quiet at the grand and stately Isabella Stewart Gardner Museum, where art lovers gazed, often in awed silence, at some of the world's most famous paintings.

The night watchman had been enjoying the peaceful evening, as he always did. The sound of the buzzer made him jump.

Then came a second buzz, this one longer.

Then a third.

Someone wanted to come in. From the quick bursts of the buzzer, that someone wanted to come in quickly. The watchman stood from his comfortable chair and stretched.

The irritating buzzing was coming from the door employees used. "Who on Earth could it be at this hour?" he thought to himself as he walked carefully across the polished floors through a wide hallway lined with paintings. He unlocked the door.

It was March 18, 1990. Ever since that night, the night watchman has regretted he ever stood from his chair.

The Isabella Stewart Gardner Museum is home to some of the most valuable paintings in the world. The museum opened in 1903, and it has attracted a steady stream of art lovers since.

Isabella Stewart Gardner began collecting famous paintings shortly after she inherited a large amount of money. In a very short time, she had so many paintings that she and her husband decided to share them with the public. They opened the museum and filled it with art from their collection. After Isabella Stewart Gardner died in 1924, she left a million dollars to the museum to keep it open to everyone who wanted to see her collection.

People came from all over the world to study the paintings by the great masters, including Vermeer, Botticelli, and Rembrandt. Many considered the Isabella Stewart Gardner Museum one of the best places in the world to sit quietly on a hallway bench and look at amazing paintings and objects. These were created as early as ancient Greece more than 2,000 years ago, right up until the 1800s. The 15-room museum was quite large, taking up almost an entire city block in Boston. You could spend a week viewing the collections and still not see everything.

Little did the night watchman know that, early on the morning of March 18, 1990, his life, and the history of the museum, was about to change dramatically.

The watchman breathed a sigh of relief as he swung open the heavy door. There, he saw two Boston policemen in their neat blue uniforms standing on the stone stoop.

Both officers had mustaches and dark hair that edged just over the tops of their ears, in the fashion of the day. One was wearing glasses. Neither one was smiling. They wore hats to protect them from the harsh March winds.

The night watchman was puzzled. Why would police be at the door, especially at this late hour?

The policemen were very formal and polite, even businesslike. They told the watchman they had come to the museum because someone had called about a disturbance. Well, the night watchman thought, if there was a disturbance somewhere in the Gardner Museum, it was a good thing the police were there to settle things down.

The first policeman stepped inside the door without being asked. The second policeman came inside, too, without looking at the watchman. They calmly walked down the front hallway as the night watchman followed.

When they reached the front desk, the first policeman turned to the watchman and asked him to call the second guard, who was inside, walking the hallways. The first watchman did not think it was unusual that the police knew about the second guard. He didn't think to ask them how they knew. He simply obeyed their request.

When the second guard arrived, the quiet and polite tone of the policemen suddenly changed. The policemen snatched the guards' arms and tied them up so quickly the guards were too shocked even to move. To make sure the watchmen were not going anywhere, the policemen handcuffed them. Then they announced:

"Gentlemen, this is a robbery."

Aha! The two men dressed as policemen were not policemen at all. The robbers led the two guards downstairs to the dark, musty basement and shoved them inside. As the guards heard the snap of the lock on the door as it closed them in, they probably worried that they had not been very good guards.

The two thieves walked calmly upstairs. They began cutting paintings away from the ornate frames where they had been gently secured hundreds of years before.

No alarms rang. No one was around to watch. With the guards locked up in the basement, the thieves had the rest of the evening to take whatever they wanted.

They were rough as they pulled frames from walls, smashed the protective glass, and cut the paintings out. They did not seem to care about how fragile the paintings were—they cared only about how much money they were worth.

And that was millions and millions of dollars.

From the damage they left behind, it was a frenzy of activity. It must have looked as though they performed delicate brain surgery with a dull butter knife.

The frames that held the paintings were themselves works of art, lavish and finely crafted by hand, and worth a lot of money. But that did not seem to matter to the thieves. They smashed the frames to get the artwork, threw the shattered splinters on the polished floors, and cut out the canvas paintings.

No one knows if the paintings were damaged.

That's because no one has seen the artwork since the heavy-handed operation. At least, no one outside of the gang that stole them has seen the paintings again.

The thieves sliced a very rare painting by the Dutch master Vermeer from its frame. Called *The Concert*, this painting was nearly as old as the works by Rembrandt down the hall.

The Concert, by Vermeer

The thieves stole three paintings by Rembrandt, the famous Dutch artist from the 1600s. These were *Storm on the Sea of Galilee*, *A Lady and Gentleman in Black*, and a portrait that the master had painted of himself.

They kept going. They lifted a painting by Govaert Flinck called *Landscape with an Obelisk*, which also was painted in the 1600s. Since they had plenty of time with the guards tied up in the basement and no alarms to worry about, the two thieves also ripped out five paintings by the famous French artist Edgar Degas. Another was from a French artist named Edouard Manet, titled *Chez Tortoni*, which he had painted in 1880.

While they were at it, they took a Chinese vase and some smaller objects, such as an ornament from the tip of a flagpole that had been used by the famous French emperor Napoleon Bonaparte about 200 years earlier. For the two thieves, the evening must have felt like a shopping spree at a very expensive store.

By the time they left, the two fake policemen had walked out with 13 pieces of very famous, extremely valuable art. When stunned museum officials sat down later to figure out what they had lost and how much it was worth, they came up with an estimate that was close to $500 million. A half a billion dollars!

The two thieves had pulled off the biggest art heist in history.

For the rest of the night, the famous Gardner Museum was as quiet as it always was. But it was a different type of silence. This time, the silence had settled around 13 empty spots on the walls. It lay on the pieces of the splintered frames strewn across the floors of hallways.

The only noises in the stately Isabella Stewart Gardner Museum for the rest of the night were the mumbles and the banging of the two handcuffed guards trapped in the basement.

At seven the next morning, nearly six hours after the surprise buzzing at the side door, a maintenance worker stepped inside to begin his usual sweeping of the wide hallways. He was shocked at what he saw. It looked as if something had exploded in the building overnight.

There was broken glass everywhere. Bits and pieces of frames littered about the once-shiny hallway floors.

Even more shocking were the empty spaces where the famous art had once hung so gracefully.

He ran to a phone in a nearby office and called the police. They responded immediately, arriving at the front door of the Gardner Museum within minutes. A problem at the Gardner Museum was always cause for concern. When the first detectives arrived, they walked slowly through the chaotic scene in stunned silence, not sure of what they were seeing or what had happened.

Then they got to work.

First, they found the two night watchmen tied up in the basement.

Next, the lead detective called the museum director and asked her to come immediately. When she arrived and saw what had happened to her beloved museum, she stared open-mouthed at the damage, so stunned she could not talk. She sat down on a hallway bench and tried not to cry.

The police called the FBI. This was more than just a small robbery. Soon, the word spread and Boston's newspapers and radio and television stations were blaring the news. The biggest art robbery in history had just occurred in Boston. Soon, the entire city and then the rest of the country were buzzing.

Once the shock had worn off and the museum officials realized the enormity of what had happened, they offered a reward of $1 million to whoever could find the art and return it. Later, they raised the amount to $5 million. It did no good.

More than anything, the museum officials worried that the art had been damaged. From the look of the shattered glass and pieces of broken frames on the hallway floors, it seemed that whoever the thieves were, they were not sensitive art lovers.

They did not know what they were looking at when they went on their stealing rampage. They did not care about preserving the work and keeping it safe.

The thieves had left many valuable pieces of art hanging on the walls—did they not realize the value of these pieces? Did they have instructions to take only certain ones? Did they have any idea what they were doing?

It was quickly apparent to police that the two thieves were working for a larger group. They were just the hired hands. Maybe someone had shown them photographs from art books of the Rembrandt and Vermeer before they dressed up as policemen and rang the buzzer that night.

They probably would not have known the difference between a famous painting and a postcard.

Another thing about stealing art—an art thief can't display their stolen paintings. The art that was stolen from the Gardner Museum was far too well-known to sell on the open market. Art thieves can't advertise their stolen goods—they'd get caught immediately.

In the world of art, or at least in the secret underworld of art, there are many wealthy private collectors who would pay a fortune to own a

Rembrandt or a Vermeer or even a piece of a flag pole once used by Napoleon. In the secret underworld of art lovers, many people would kill to be the only ones in the room to sit and admire a rare and beautiful painting by a Dutch master. They don't mind stealing from a museum or from the millions of other art lovers who no longer get a chance for such a view.

The police and FBI agents studied the scene. They looked for fingerprints and small things the thieves might have left behind by accident. They took hundreds of photographs. They asked a million questions.

When a museum has nearly half a billion dollars in world-famous art stolen, it is not a matter to be taken lightly.

The FBI began a search that eventually spread around the world. The search stretched across the Atlantic Ocean to Great Britain and involved the famous Scotland Yard. It moved on to France and around the other side of the world to Japan.

Their efforts led nowhere.

While the FBI followed the rumors about the stolen artwork from England to France to Japan, the evidence has come to show that the trail was actually much closer to Boston. It pointed first to nearby Connecticut, where the FBI believes the art was briefly hidden. Then the stolen paintings were moved farther down Interstate 95 to Philadelphia, Pennsylvania.

The FBI thinks that the largest art heist in history was planned and organized by a man named Robert Gentile. He sometimes went by the nickname "Bobby the Cook." Robert Gentile had been involved in organized crime for many years in Philadelphia and Connecticut.

The FBI knew that his nickname had nothing to do with delicious food and more to do with the ideas for crimes he cooked up.

The FBI heard Robert Gentile mention the art in a telephone conversation. They also found a list of all the artworks and what they were worth in Robert Gentile's house. The FBI thinks that Robert Gentile knows where the art is. Or, that at least he could send them in the right direction to find wherever it has been hidden for all these years.

They have gone to Robert Gentile's house in Connecticut a number of times and dug up his backyard, looking for clues—or maybe even the art. The FBI has been very thorough in its searches. During the latest attempt, the FBI brought 15 cars and three large trucks and heavy equipment. They spent all day digging. Nothing.

Today, Robert Gentile is an old man and in poor health. At least they know where he is—in prison waiting for a trial for other crimes. Robert Gentile says that he does not know a thing about the art or what happened on March 18, 1990. He wishes the FBI would stop bothering him.

But the FBI will not give up.

Robert Gentile is steadfast in saying he had nothing to do with the theft, even with all the evidence that has piled up against him. The man is still not talking, and no one knows why.

Robert Gentile might very well take his secrets to the grave.

WHAT ELSE WAS HAPPENING IN 1990?

- David Dinkins is sworn in as the first African American mayor of New York City.

- The famous Leaning Tower of Pisa is closed down for safety reasons. Why? It was leaning too much.

- The first McDonald's in Russia opens in Moscow. It is also the world's biggest McDonald's.

- South African President F.W. de Klerk announces that Nelson Mandela is a free man and releases him from prison near Cape Town. Mandela was held for 27 years for fighting the government's racial policies of apartheid.

- Art is also in the news in New York City, where a portrait by Vincent van Gogh sells at auction for $82.5 million.

- Muppets creator Jim Henson, famous for creating the *Sesame Street* characters Ernie and Bert, Oscar the Grouch, Grover, Cookie Monster, and Big Bird, dies at the age of 54.

- The Hubble Space Telescope sends back its first photos from space.

- The popular television show *Seinfeld* makes its debut.

- The temperature rockets to 122 degrees in Phoenix, Arizona.

- Smoking on airplanes is banned.

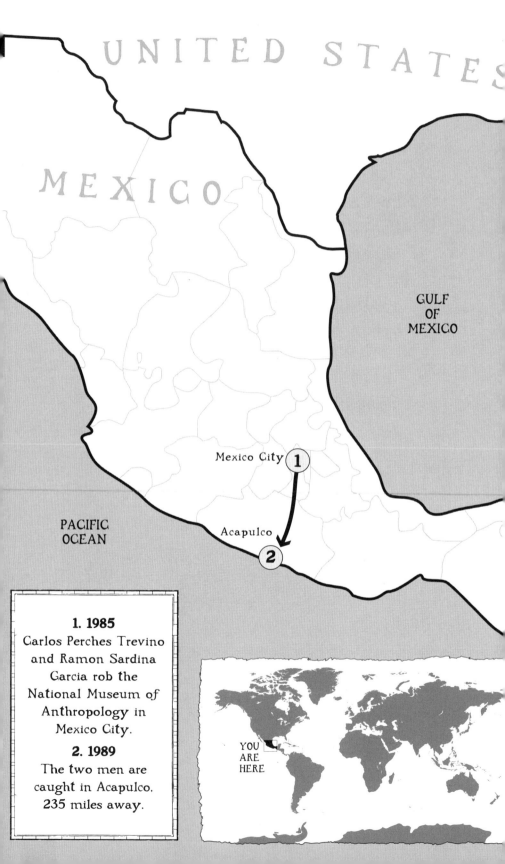

UNITED STATES

MEXICO

GULF
OF
MEXICO

PACIFIC
OCEAN

Mexico City ①

Acapulco

②

1. 1985
Carlos Perches Trevino
and Ramon Sardina
Garcia rob the
National Museum of
Anthropology in
Mexico City.

2. 1989
The two men are
caught in Acapulco,
235 miles away.

YOU
ARE
HERE

Chapter Five

The Heist that Hurt
an Entire Country

When they were boys, Carlos Perches
Trevino and Ramon Sardina Garcia loved
animals. Both were crazy about every
animal you could think of. Dogs or cats,
wild or tame, big or small, furry, scaly, or
bald—it didn't matter to these boys.

As they grew up in bustling Mexico City, they
were so infatuated with animals that they
worked hard in high school and enrolled in
veterinary school. It was the early 1980s and
they both wanted to learn as much as they
could about the animals they adored.

Except—studying veterinary medicine was not
what they had expected.

83

Carlos Perches Trevino and Ramon Sardina Garcia met in classes with names such as "Mammalian Physiology" and "Comparative Anatomy of Vertebrates." They noticed each other staring out the windows of the classroom while the teacher lectured about the details of the nervous systems of platypuses and penguins. During long laboratory sessions, when they were supposed to be creating chemical reactions, one or the other would sometimes nod off at the table.

Veterinary school was very hard, much harder than high school. Keeping up with classes required a lot more work than either of them wanted to do. Classes and the constant studying were a rude awakening. They quickly learned that studying veterinary medicine was not a walk in the park.

Loving animals was not enough to get them through vet school.

Being at the bottom of the class gave Carlos Perches Trevino and Ramon Sardina Garcia something in common. Soon, they began to talk and get to know each other. They became good friends.

After talking late into the night, they discovered something else they both liked—maybe even more than animals. They both loved money. And they both hated working for it. They talked for hours about how to get a lot of money with as little work as possible.

They dreamed of being rich, and hoped it would not take too much time or work.

It was only a matter of time before they learned of the popular National Museum of Anthropology near their veterinary school in Mexico City. The museum sat quietly between Paseo de la Reforma and Mahatma Gandhi Street in beautiful Chapultepec Park. It was one of the biggest city parks in the world.

The National Museum of Anthropology was a modern building, quite large and very attractive. It had 23 rooms that held the most valuable artifacts from Mexico's impressive history. At its center, the museum had a wide courtyard with a pond, and it was ringed by gardens with exhibits, both inside and out. The grounds of the museum covered nearly 20 acres—about the size of five city blocks.

The size of the museum and its quiet setting soon played an important part in their plan. Carlos Perches Trevino and Ramon Sardina Garcia began to hatch this plan while they should have been studying veterinary medicine.

One day, after a short visit to the museum, the two talked about what they had seen there. Everything on display had been carefully collected to show visitors how sophisticated and advanced their earlier culture had been.

Enter the museum and you first notice the huge Sun Stone, a calendar stretching 11 feet across. The Sun Stone had been carved in basalt by Aztecs. The Aztec Empire, which ruled Mexico in the 1500s, was one of the most developed in the world, and the Sun Stone is just one example of their scientific knowledge. The massive calendar weighs about 24 tons and is remarkably accurate.

Walk farther down the halls of the National Museum of Anthropology and you'll see rings, carvings shaped like bats, masks, and more jewelry from the Aztecs. The artifacts are so impressive that people from around Mexico visit the museum to see the work of their ancestors.

You'll also find ceremonial masks from the Maya empire, which reached its peak between the second and the fifth centuries. They built beautiful cities and studied astronomy and mathematics long before much of the rest of the world.

Visitors looked at the objects of art closely. They imagined the people who made them and what they were doing so many years before. For many Mexicans, a trip to the National Museum of Anthropology was a time of discovery and learning and great national pride.

Carlos Perches Trevino and Ramon Sardina Garcia noticed something beyond the delicacy of the carvings and historic importance of the objects on display. They saw that many of the items were made of valuable gold and turquoise and jade.

The objects on display were worth a lot of money—millions of dollars. One of the most popular displays was a vase shaped like a monkey that was worth $20 million. And there were many more objects just like this vase, displayed invitingly close to visitors.

Carlos Perches Trevino and Ramon Sardina Garcia might have had their fair share of pride in their Mexican heritage. But after their visits to the museum, they were more excited about the amount of money all of the artifacts were worth.

Let's rob the museum, they decided.

Soon after their first visit, they started paying much more attention to the museum than they had to boring lectures about the digestive system of elephants. The two young men who were too lazy to open their textbooks and study began to learn everything they could about the museum.

If they had put the same amount of effort into their study of veterinary medicine, they would have graduated at the top of their class.

One of the first things they decided was that they would not be taking the Sun Stone. It would be too hard to roll it out of the museum without anyone noticing. Most of the other objects were quite small—small enough to stick in a bag and carry out. They knew it would be easy to grab and walk out with the $20-million monkey-shaped vase.

The Sun Stone
credit: Arian Zwegers, CC by 2.0

Not bad money for something that fit into a backpack. Now all they needed was a good plan for getting into the museum.

They started skipping classes and spending their days at Chapultepec Park. It's an area of the busy city where Aztec royalty had once gathered to relax. They needed a place to get away from the tensions of running their huge empire hundreds of years ago.

The Aztecs had ruled for close to 100 years. Like the Maya before them, the Aztecs had a sophisticated system of laws. They built grand temples with engineering skills no one in the rest of the Americas had developed yet.

By 1985, when Carlos Perches Trevino and Ramon Sardina Garcia started thinking about their heist, thousands of people strolled through Chapultepec Park every day. They enjoyed the fresh air and the warm sunshine. Like the Aztecs, they visited to escape the tensions of life in the big city.

Because Chapultepec Park was so huge and popular, and because the National Museum of Anthropology drew so many people through its doors to see the Sun Stone and other objects, it was very easy for Carlos Perches Trevino and Ramon Sardina Garcia to blend in and not be noticed. People were there to look at the art, not at the visitors.

This was a good thing, because from July until December of 1985, the young men made 50 visits to the museum.

Each time the men visited, they looked for clues to how they could rob the museum and not be caught. They studied different ways to get in and out of the museum without being seen.

Lost in the crowds, they took photographs of doors and windows. They studied locks and latches. They looked very closely at the glass-and-wood display cases that held some of the world's most valuable objects.

The objects inside sat so close and appeared to be so flimsily protected. It seemed almost as if they were begging to be stolen.

Carlos Perches Trevino and Ramon Sardina Garcia made maps of trails around the museum in Chapultepec Park and of the paths they could use to escape with the stolen treasures. They drew diagrams of hallways. They studied the guards and their habits and learned when the guards patrolled the museum and when they sat.

Soon, they knew where the guards rested and for how long. It was all part of the plan that was beginning to form. Carlos Perches Trevino and Ramon Sardina Garcia were very thorough.

The two students who could not stay awake in class suddenly had a lot of energy. Apparently, millions of dollars can be a major motivator.

After six months of planning the heist, the pair realized it would be fairly easy to sneak into the National Museum of Anthropology at night, after the doors were closed to the public. They could simply get in through one of the air-conditioning vents.

The vents were covered inside and out by thin screens. All they had to do was pry off the screens, crawl a short distance through the vent, and pop off the screen on the inside. There they would be—inside the National Museum of Anthropology—with a fortune right at their fingertips.

On Christmas Eve in 1985, Carlos Perches Trevino and Ramon Sardina Garcia decided it was time. Maybe they joked about giving themselves a very big Christmas present.

That night, acting as if nothing big was about to happen, Carlos Perches Trevino and Ramon Sardina Garcia spent the evening with their families celebrating the holiday. They joked with their parents and teased their brothers and sisters. Then, they each said goodbye to their families and changed into black clothing, better for blending into the darkness.

They met outside Carlos Perches Trevino's house and he drove them in his Volkswagen Bug to Chapultepec Park. They quietly rolled to a stop outside the National Museum of Anthropology. Inside, waiting for them, was millions of dollars in rare artifacts, theirs for the taking.

Soon, they realized they'd been given another Christmas gift. Once they crawled through the vent and popped open the screen inside, everything was very still. No guards seemed to be patrolling. The guards were all at a party! It was Christmas Eve, after all. They could hear singing and laughter from a room on the other side of the museum.

Carlos Perches Trevino and Ramon Sardina Garcia had the whole museum to themselves while the guards drank and sang Christmas carols, paying no attention to whatever else was going on in the quiet museum hallways.

Still, Carlos Perches Trevino and Ramon Sardina Garcia worked quickly. After so many months of studying, they knew what they wanted and they went after it efficiently and with great glee. All their planning was about to pay off.

Very carefully and quietly, so they would not alert the singing guards, they walked to a display case, pried off the wooden molding that held the protective glass in place, reached in, and helped themselves. They lifted a Mayan mask made of precious jade, then some valuable ornaments from the tomb of an Aztec king.

They smiled as they worked. It was all so easy. In a little more than half an hour, they lifted 124 pieces of valuable art. Many of the pieces they pilfered were made of gold. As they worked their way down the line of cases, they put each item into a canvas suitcase they had brought along.

They never heard a guard the entire time.

When the canvas bag was filled, they retraced their steps and crawled back through the vent to the outside. As they left, they heard the guards, still singing and laughing. Then, they walked slowly back to the car and drove from Chapultepec Park.

No one had noticed a thing.

Carlos Perches Trevino and Ramon Sardina Garcia had pulled off the biggest and most outrageous heist in the history of Mexico. It went off without a hitch. The two students were now among the most successful thieves in the world.

Carlos Perches Trevino returned to his apartment with the full suitcase and hid it in his closet. The pair talked and agreed it would be best to leave the art in the closet until things cooled down. They were fairly certain there would be some sort of fuss when the theft was discovered.

They did not know just how big the fuss would be, though.

Their devious work was not discovered until five hours later, when a new shift of guards arrived and began making their morning rounds. After the new guards saw the empty display cases, the news spread like a wildfire in a dry forest. That can happen when national treasures have been stolen, treasures that have been the source of such national pride to so many.

Immediately after the news of the theft was announced, the entire country reeled in shock. An alarm went out from the president of Mexico to almost every person in every corner of the country. Carlos Perches Trevino and Ramon Sardina Garcia had done more than steal some gold and jade. They had insulted an entire nation.

Their theft was a tremendous insult to the millions of Mexicans who valued their Mayan and Aztec cultures.

Who would do such a callous and unthinking thing? Everyone demanded that the art be found and found quickly. It had to be located before it was damaged or sold to a private collector and never seen in public again.

Police jumped into action the second they heard about the theft. They ordered that thousands of miles of border be closed. Ships leaving port were searched, cars and trucks were stopped at border crossings, and airline passengers were frisked. The police put up posters all over the country and closed railroad stations. They were convinced that the theft must have been the work of a sophisticated international ring of thieves.

The Mexican police asked for help from police in other countries, calling around the world to get fingerprints of well-known art thieves.

They asked on national television that everyone in the country be on the lookout for anything suspicious. Museum officials announced a large reward for information that led to the return of the stolen goods.

Not knowing that two poor veterinary students were really the ones behind the heist, police arrested the 10 guards who had been singing and partying at the museum on Christmas Eve. It would take days before the guards were cleared of all charges.

While the search for the stolen artifacts spread around the world, the canvas bag full of stolen art sat right in the heart of Mexico City in Carlos Perches Trevino's closet. The two thieves had not thought about how to find a buyer for the artifacts they'd stolen.

They had not considered how difficult it would be to sell a national treasure.

The artifacts they had stolen were the most recognizable pieces of art in the entire country of Mexico. After the theft was announced, newspapers and television stations had shown photographs of the missing pieces. No one in the dark underworld of criminals who might normally buy stolen goods wanted any part of the National Museum of Anthropology heist.

Dealing with that theft was an invitation to a long prison sentence. The goods were too hot— even the most hardened criminal wanted nothing to do with them. Carlos Perches Trevino and Ramon Sardina Garcia had not thought about any of this.

The canvas bag and the millions of dollars worth of stolen artifacts sat in the closet for more than a year, untouched and unsold. Then, Carlos Perches Trevino had an idea. They would move to the Mexican city of Acapulco, which had a reputation for being a bit wild. They talked themselves into believing that they could find a buyer in Acapulco.

Soon enough, they fell in with a tough crowd of criminals—men and women who robbed banks and sold illegal drugs. Carlos Perches Trevino and Ramon Sardina Garcia hoped that among their new and questionable friends was someone who would know how to unload the art.

Of course, becoming friends with robbers and drug dealers has its dangers. Carlos Perches Trevino hired a drug dealer to sell the artifacts, offering to split any profits from a sale.

But it was a mistake to think that a drug dealer would know where to sell the artifacts. While Carlos Perches Trevino and Ramon Sardina Garcia thought they had made friends with the right people, they instead had stepped into a very big pile of trouble.

The two young men were not good students at veterinary school and they were not good students of the world of crime.

Shortly after the drug dealer promised to sell the artifacts from the National Museum of Anthropology, he was arrested. It took no time at all for the drug dealer to tell the police that if they gave him a break, he would lead them to the stolen artifacts.

On June 15, 1989, more than three years after the Christmas Eve theft, police raided Carlos Perches Trevino's apartment. They arrested him for the crime that had broken the heart of an entire country. The stolen goods were still in the canvas bag where they had been placed years before. Ramon Sardina Garcia was arrested later.

The biggest theft in Mexican history had been solved. The two young men were about to learn that prison was much harder than studying veterinary medicine.

When the news was announced that the thieves had been caught, the entire country celebrated. National pride was restored. The president of Mexico smiled broadly as he stood in front of the stolen artifacts before they were returned to the National Museum of Anthropology.

Then, he announced that the museum would be adding more guards with more training, cameras, special alarms, and extra security at the National Museum of Anthropology.

There has never been a theft there again.

WHAT ELSE WAS HAPPENING IN 1985?

- An 8.1 Richter scale earthquake strikes Mexico City, killing more than 9,000 people.

- 14-year-old Mary Joe Fernandez becomes the youngest player to win a tennis match at the U.S. Open in August.

- Coca-Cola introduces a new formula for its popular drink, calling it "New Coke." No one likes it and the company later switches back to the original formula.

- Scientists in Great Britain announce they have discovered a hole in the ozone layer of the earth's atmosphere.

- Microsoft introduces Windows 1.0.

- Robert Penn Warren is named the first American poet laureate.

accomplice: a helper in a crime.

ally: a loyal friend who supports a cause.

ambition: a desire for achievement or distinction such as power, honor, fame, or wealth.

ancestry: the family and culture you come from.

anthropology: the study of humans and how they developed—from cave dwellers to today.

apartheid: a set of laws made by the white rulers of the Republic of South Africa that sorted citizens by color and race and favored people with white skin. It was ended in 1994.

artifact: an object made by people in the past, including tools, pottery, and jewelry.

ascent: a path rising through the air.

astronomy: the study of the stars, planets, and space.

audacious: bold behavior beyond what people think of as normal.

bail: a sum of money given to be temporarily released from jail. It is to guarantee that person's appearance in court.

bravura: great skill and brilliance shown in a performance or activity.

bribe: a gift, often money, to get someone to do something wrong and often illegal.

callous: hard and without sympathy; not feeling any concern about the sufferings of other people.

candelabra: a large fancy candleholder or light fixture.

caper: a dangerous activity, especially one involving robbery.

ceremonial: using formal actions to celebrate or honor an event.

civilization: a community of people that is advanced in art, science, and government.

climate: the average weather patterns in an area during a long period of time.

Glossary

composite: combining two or more images to make a single picture.

coincidence: when events happen together in ways that make it seem like they were planned together.

culture: the beliefs and way of life of a group of people.

cultured: having good manners and a good education.

deteriorate: to rot or become worse.

dignity: being worthy of honor or respect.

disciplined: the ability to behave calmly and stay in control, even when it is hard to do so.

disband: to break up as a group or a gang.

district attorney: an elected or appointed official who represents the government when prosecuting a crime.

engineer: the driver of a railroad locomotive; also, a person who uses science, math, and creativity to design and build things.

engineering: the use of science and math in the design and construction of things.

exotic: unusual and colorful.

exploit: a daring event.

eyewitness: a person who sees an act or event and can give a firsthand account of it.

flamboyant: showy and flashy, like wearing a hat with feathers or neon-yellow pants. Flamboyant people are not shy.

forensic scientist: an expert who analyzes and explains evidence found at a crime scene using chemical and physical analysis.

forger: a skilled artist or craftsman who can make a fake copy of something look so real it can be sold as the original for a lot of money.

frenzy: an out-of-control action.

frustrated: a feeling of annoyance and anger when you are prevented from moving forward.

fuselage: the main body of an aircraft.

guise: putting on an outward appearance and pretending to be something you are not—usually to trick people.

heist: a robbery.

hijack: to illegally seize a ship, aircraft, or vehicle and force it to go to a different destination.

immigrant: a newcomer to a country.

infatuated: almost goofy with love and passion for something, usually, but not always, another person.

infiltrate: to join a group to spy on it or to sneak into a place to get information.

intelligence: the ability to acquire knowledge and skills.

knapsack: a backpack.

landscape: a large area of land and its features, such as mountains and rivers.

lavish: more than what people expect.

mastermind: the main planner of a complicated plan, such as a bank or train robbery.

mountainous: covered in mountains or very large.

obsidian: black volcanic glass formed by the rapid cooling of lava.

ornate: fancy, almost more than necessary to make something look good.

ozone: a gas in the upper atmosphere that forms a layer around the planet. The ozone layer protects the planet from the sun's most damaging rays and helps keep the planet a comfortable temperature.

peddler: a person who sells things, often on the street from carts or tables. Usually the goods are used or not very well made, but they are inexpensive.

phenomenon: someone or something that is really special; often used to describe an athlete or a singer.

pickpocket: a thief who steals from pockets or bags, usually in public places where people are not paying attention.

Glossary

porcelain: a shiny and hard material used for making plates and cups. Some porcelain is valuable.

precaution: setting up protection ahead of time. Putting on sunscreen before you walk across the Sahara Desert is a precaution.

rampage: uncontrolled and usually violent behavior.

ransom: a payment demanded in exchange for releasing a captive.

reign: the period of time a ruler rules.

routine: the regular sequence of events.

saloon: usually a rough and tough place to drink alcohol, favored by people who don't like fancy restaurants where they have to dress up.

seamy: rough and unpleasant.

sensational: an event, person, or piece of information that causes great public interest and excitement.

slaughterhouse: a place to butcher animals.

sophisticated: polished and smart and polite.

stately: impressive and dignified.

stealthy: quiet, sneaky.

stonemason: a skilled person who builds and fixes things made of stone.

suave: charming and confident.

theory: an idea that could explain how or why something happens.

throng: a large crowd of people, sometimes out of control.

underworld: the world of criminals or of organized crime.

uptown: toward the northern part of a city. In New York City today, it means above 59th Street.

wily: clever and sly and, more often than not, sneaky.

wits: smarts and brainpower.

Yiddish: a Jewish language based on German but with many other influences.

D.B. Cooper Records:
vault.fbi.gov/D-B-Cooper%20

You can read the FBI records that were kept on D.B. Cooper. These records were collected between 1971 and 1992.

D.B. Cooper Development:
washingtonpost.com/news/post-nation/wp/2017/01/16/
the-d-b-cooper-case-baffled-investigators-for-decades-
now-scientists-have-a-new-theory

Read an article about a 2017 development in the D.B. Cooper case.

School for Common Thieves:
atlasobscura.com/articles/new-yorks-first-female-crime-
boss-started-her-own-crime-school

Read more about Marm Mandelbaum's school for common thieves and see some of the cartoons that were drawn about her.

Great Train Robbery Obituary:
telegraph.co.uk/news/obituaries/12129733/Gordon-
Goody-Great-Train-Robber-obituary.html

Read the obituary of one of the masterminds of the Great Train Robbery and see photos of the people and places involved in the robbery.

Tour the Isabella Stewart Gardner Museum:
gardnermuseum.org/resources/theft

Using Google Maps, you can tour the Isabella Stewart Gardner Museum and see the empty frames that still hang on the walls, waiting for their paintings to be returned.